SOUNDBYTES

SOUNDBYTES

MAGNOLIA SAGE

PARTRIDGE

Print information available on the last page.

To order additional copies of this book, contact
Toll Free 800 101 2657 (Singapore)
Toll Free 1 800 81 7340 (Malaysia)
orders.singapore@partridgepublishing.com

www.partridgepublishing.com/singapore

Eros

My dearest love whom I adore muchly

This is a look into my mind, you probably know what my thoughts are like; I am pretty vocal with what I think and you are kinda smart sometimes.

Some of this will be hard to read, that is because I am writing this at a tough phase of my life.

I was considering not sharing this with you until things are better, because of how hard it was writing and how hard it still is reading what I wrote, who knows I might actually change my mind.

I believe you when you say that you still care for me, but I can not believe that you stopped loving me, you might not love me the way I love you but you still love me.

I hope that I was not too much trouble to have around, and i hope we can make it work again.

I hope that you can manage to get over your troubles and insecurities. Maybe then you will see that it is okay for me to love you as much as i do, and that it is okay for you to accept my love (if you want).

Hopefully in time we can be okay with ourselves and each other, enough to consider trying again and attempting to make it work.

Eros

Crescendo

If I told you any of this you will start crying.
you ask me how i am and i reply that i am okay,
you insist on knowing how i feel,
I ask you what do you think you reply with upset and confused.

I am upset and confused
I am also upset because I feel betrayed and lied to
how could i have been so stupid to not see that you were done
done using me
all you wanted was to leave

You say you didn't love me
you just liked that i made you feel special
so you let me stay

Once I started asking for a commitment
not even like i have just a little
so i did not feel like i was wasting my time

I gave you everything
you could not

Crescendo

My tears have dried
My blood is drying
I am still all alone
Nowhere to go
Nothing to do

Eros

My tears have dried,
So
The sky is crying instead of me.

Iota

I hope to get my
Self confidence back before
It is
Too late

Crescendo

You insist on talking
But
You do not say
Anything

Idiote

God
Does not
Love
Me

Eros

Iota

Please
Do
Not
Blink

I am sorry for the
Harmful things that I said.
I always talked to you from
My heart, and my heart
Is still hurting.

Crescendo

All I want to do is
Either cry or scream.

Idiote

God
Does not
Love
Me

Eros

Your gorgeous soul
Your mind that would challenge
And entertain mine.
Your luscious lips, that skin
That is as sooth as the
Purest silk.
Your eyes that would knock
Me out if you'd just blink.

Iota

I hope that I will be able
To leave you when the time
Comes, right now you can't
Accept my love and time
Apart might be good for
Both of us.

Crescendo

Right now I just put
My hope and faith in
God then
Myself

Idiote

If I
Say I am
Okay
I will get
Worse

Eros

You are too beautiful to
Let go so easily.
You are too beautiful to
Let go.

Iota

I want you to feel the
Way I feel when I am
With you, even if it was
Just a fraction of it.
(That is why I want you
to experience the sunrise
at the beach)

Crescendo

Never
Wanted
Always
Used

Idiote

If I admit to
Getting worse
They will want
To take me
Away

Eros

I fear what the future holds,
I am excited for the surprises
But what I think is
Coming terrifies me.

Iota

I also hope that by
Leaving I can give myself
The chance to grow and heal.

Crescendo

You brought the happiest
And darkest thoughts that
Crossed my mind.

Idiote

I survived
I struggled
I am done surviving
I am done struggling

Eros

Did you really
Stop
Loving
Me

Iota

I hate dealing with
Needy people because
They remind me of
Myself

Crescendo

I am tired, I am real close
To giving up, nothing matters
And I can't have you.

Idiote

I
Do not
Want to be
Saved

Eros

When I used to see you smile,
My heart would dance, my lungs
Would fail, and I would
Lose my mind.
I felt like I was dying
And I loved it.

Iota

Hey there dearly kind hearted,
It is not your fault they stopped
Loving you, keep getting stronger
And stay beautiful.
Someday someone will love
You enough to want to stay,
Or they will want your love
And they will be able to
Accept it. If you are lucky
They can be the same person
If you are really lucky
You'll get to kiss them.

Crescendo

I love you enough to wait
Around forever, would you
Do the same?

Idiote

Nothing
To live for
Nothing
To die for

Eros

I
Love
You.

Iota

Peace and love
Come from within.
How will I be able to feel peace
And love when I am dead inside,
How can I not feel the urge to
Match how I feel inside whenever
I am not being distracted by everyday
Life.

Crescendo

I want my heart to stop hurting,
I want to sleep without crying,
I want to close my eyes without
Risking my sanity.

Idiote

Nothing
To live for
Nothing
To die for

Eros

It might be too late to
Tell you this but a lot of
This is very personal.

Iota

I am tired of being
Tired, and I have no
Idea what to do about anything
Anymore.

Crescendo

I can't leave   you don't want me
I can't go   you don't need me
I can't move   you don't love me
I can't stay   you don't
                       You just don't

Idiote

I want my
Heart
To stop hurting
Or
Just stop

Eros

My heart still beats faster
Just by the
Thought of
You.

Iota

I am being bounced around between
Specialists and consultants.
None of my caretakers know how to
Take care of me, because I do not
know how
To
Help myself.

Crescendo

Sleep is for The Sober Hearts

Idiote

You
Were all I wanted
Before I knew I
wanted
You.

Maybe when I am no longer
A patient I could learn
To be more
Patient.

Iota

I have a lot of faith in God,
Even when I believe that he does
Not love me. God rewards
Those who ask. I have been asking
For a beautiful miracle for so long
But God does not reward those
Who lost hope.

Crescendo

I should stop thinking, all
My thoughts lead to you, and
Thinking of you hurts my heart.

Idiote

It was God,
Then you.
I lost God,
The same time
I lost you.

Eros

Being in the state that I
Am in now, I know that it
Will be extremely toxic for
Me to stay your friend. I
Am doing so because I want
To see you get better and
I want you to see me try.

Iota

You say you stopped loving
Me, I am sorry you feel that
Way, I still love you.
I love you more and more
Every moment of everyday.
I love you more than life.

Crescendo

I do not know when I got
So scared, scared to lose
You, scared to hurt you,
Scared to say something
Wrong.

Idiote

I saw the universe in your eyes
That's when I realized
You are worth
Everything

Eros

I tried to write a story
But I realized that it
Could never capture how
I felt, and I also ran out
Of patience.

Iota

I would love
To keep on trying,
But right now I am
Clueless about what I should do.

Crescendo

I want to take a
Thousand pictures of you, but
I can't not stare at you
When I am in your presence

Idiote

I hold the most respect for you,
What you did and said.
I always tried to make sure
Not to make you feel
Inferior, stupid or insignificant.
I guess we did not share
That sentiment.
I still think highly of you.

Eros

Imagining myself killing
Myself was always a
Happy thought that calmed
Me down.

Iota

Blessed with a
Beautiful brain,
But it is disintegrating because
Of my ugly thoughts.

Crescendo

Things that I should not
Do are what I
Crave
The most.

Idiote

I was broken before you came,
I was broken when you left me,
And I was still broken when you
Stopped.
For a moment
When I believed you loved me
I was okay with being broken.

Eros

Your intentions were pure,
I am sorry I misunderstood.
My intentions were pure,
I am sorry you misunderstood.
I think we know our hearts
Were gold for each other.

Iota

Maybe god is teaching me to
Fight harder for what I want,
Patience, and to appreciate
His blessing by taking away
What I held dearest to
My heart.

Crescendo

I wish you never
Hurt like I am
Hurting.

Idiote

I
Was
Faded

Eros

When I was experiencing fall
It felt like if I slept I would
Never wake up,
If I did not have you
Around I probably would
Not have experienced it hat
Bad, I also would
Have jumped.

Iota

Do not lose the enormous
Amount of strength that
You posses, build on it.
Stay beautiful.

Crescendo

I was told that I should
Want to hate you, that I
Should wish you harm, and
That I should try to hurt
You like you hurt me, but
I can't get myself to do anything
Of that sort, I wont forgive
Myself if a tear fell from your
Eyes because of me.

Idiote

I did not mean to threaten you,
I wanted to let you know that
I act irrationally
Sometimes
I'm sorry I kissed her.
I'm sorry you stopped loving
Me.

Eros

When I was experiencing fall
It felt like you did not
Care enough to try to
Help.

Iota

I might have never loved
You, I might have just been
Too afraid to lose you and
We decided to agree that
Was love.

Crescendo

I cry and scream in my
Sleep because when I sleep,
I can not control my
Bottled up emotions.

Idiote

You promised
That you will love me
So much that I will
Learn to love myself.

Eros

It is hard to talk about
Hopes and wants, when it
Feels like the whole world
And God are always working
Against you.

Iota

Touch me   want me
Tease me   take me
Love me   have me
Fuck me   keep me

Crescendo

Lost
Scared
And confused

Idiote

I felt like I setup myself
To fail in my relationships,
But not with you,
I have never wanted to
Succeed at anything as
Much as I wanted you.
I still want to spend the
Rest of my life with you.

Eros

Dealing with you leaving is
Painful, I feel like I
Gave you everything, now
That you do not love me
I feel like I ended up with
Nothing.

Iota

I am trying to feel better
About myself, I have been
Trying to do good, but nothing
Seems to be working.

Crescendo

You said that you were not
Ready to be with anyone,
I wonder if you would want
Me once you are ready, or you
Would want to peruse someone
Else.

Idiote

I tried my best to make
You happy.
I tried my best to make
You stay.
I lost myself when
I stopped making you love
Me.

Eros

I feel like I need a change,
U want to leave for a while,
Maybe for a few years, until I
Feel better, until I can
Identify with myself.

Iota

I keep on messing up, everything
I lay my hands on shatters and
Breaks, except the defenses
You put up to protect your
Gorgeous heart.

Crescendo

I realize that if you were
To want to come back I
Would not let you have me,
I am not done hurting and
I did not start healing.

Idiote

I am done
I am less than mediocre
I have no self respect
I am desperate
I do not want anything.

Eros

Putting my thoughts to
Paper is helping me find
Some ease, but
It is also helping me
Realize things I did not
Want to know.

Iota

From the first day I asked you to
Be with me, I laid myself out
For you. I told you my flaws,
My obsessions and that you will
Be one of them, my crazy rational,
My anxieties, and my insecurities.
I told you that eventually you
Would want to leave,
I told you it would not
Work out.

Crescendo

It hurts hearing you
Refer to you and I as us,
When clearly we aren't.

Idiote

I want to rest
In life
Or death
All I want is to be at
Ease

Eros

Maybe instead of being on
Different pages of the same
Book, we should have
Been writing our own
Book together.

Iota

You insisted on being with me,
You insisted on trying, you
Wanted to be the exception.
Oh god, were you the exception,
You let me love you more than
Life, then you decided you did not
Love me anymore.

Crescendo

Love,
Marriage
And other drugs.

Idiote

I obviously will not find
Peace where I am,
Here I am a fake.

Eros

You believed that we were
Toxic to each other, you
Were probably right,
I hope that one day
When we are better for
Each other and ourselves that
We could possibly try again.

Iota

I feel like I am losing it,
I feel like I am going insane
It feels like that will be
Easier to explain than
Retelling my story.

Crescendo

Weak, nothing you can do
Insignificant, nothing you can change
Worthless, nothing you can effect

Idiote

Thinking of suicide
Helps
Calm my anxiety

Eros

Iota

I lost God
I lost you
I lost myself

I have never felt like I lost
So much time and effort, not
Just time wasted but also
Time gone, things I can not
Take back or undo.

Crescendo

If things do not get better,
Wait
It
Out

Idiote

I want to die
With a glass full of Hennessey,
A cigar dipped in blue label,
And
A gun under my chin.

Eros

I remember back when talking to
You was so easy, I would say
The weirdest most bizarre shit
And I did not feel like you
Judged me.
Now I am scared to say hello.

Iota

I have never experienced
Such sorrow
I have never felt
Such despair

Crescendo

Things will get better
If not soon
Hopefully
Eventually

Idiote

Never
Good
Enough

Eros

I feel like it I did not
Try so hard I would have
Had some energy left
To do something now.

Iota

You said that we can
Make it work,
Seems like you convinced me
But you couldn't convince
Yourself.

Crescendo

It is okay to not be okay.
It is okay to be happy.
It is okay to accept the good
That life is offering you.
It is okay to ask for something
That you want.
It is okay that I still love you.
It is okay.

Idiote

I am mentally
Ill
And emotionally unstable

Eros

Now that you are gone I
Can get wasted, fuck everyone
And not feel any
Guilt

Iota

You allowed me to open up and
Give you everything,
It is a shame you couldn't
Allow yourself to do the same.

Crescendo

Idiote

I have no priority in your life
And that is obvious,
You always had better things
To do and other people to
Talk to.
It's a shame I was not
One of them and that
I was just there for you
When you had nothing better
To do.

Eros

For now I just wish to
Be okay with myself, enough
So I can stop feeling so
Worthless.

Iota

You held your defenses high
And strong.
I did not know how to
Break through because I
Was afraid of hurting you.

Crescendo

Learn to love who
You are and
You will be who
You want to be.

Idiote

You called me desperate and
Said that I had no
Self respect for trying to
Make you stay.
Thank you for stating the
Obvious and
I am sorry for loving
You as much as I do.

Eros

I promised to always love you,
And that is a promise that
I am willing to keep.
It is difficult to keep
Loving someone who
Does not love you.

Iota

You protected your heart and
Broke mine.
You probably did not mean
To but it was an unfortunate
Consequence.

Crescendo

Learn to love yourself
Before you try to
Love anyone
Else.

Idiote

It feels like you do not really
Want me around, feels like
You are letting me stay
In case you change your mind
Again.

Eros

I once called you a distraction
From killing myself, even thought
That is true but
For what it is worth
You are more than a distraction.

Iota

More than sometimes
I just want to
Jump.

My wellbeing is not that
Important to me right now,
All I want is to get
Drunk.

Idiote

I
Want
To rest

Eros

I hope that I can regain my
Confidence. I want to feel
Good about myself, my insecurities
Would probably be around but
I will be strong enough to
Be okay with them.

Iota

I was asked if I thought about
Death, I said yes; truth is
That I think about dying
All the time.

Crescendo

Always tired, except I can't rest
Always dreaming, except I can't sleep
Always yearning, except I can't have
Always wanting, except I can't take

Idiote

Medicine works
better
With alcohol
I want a drink
I need a drink
I deserve a drink

Eros

I feel so lost, I have no
Confidence in what I do
Anymore; I am tired of asking
For validation, acceptance, and
To be wanted, all that should
Come from myself not others.

Iota

These things do not just
Happen, you allowed
It to happen.

Crescendo

When you left, you left a
Void that so far no amount
Of booze, cigars and girls
Could fill.

Idiote

Alcohol makes me feel
Like I do not want
To die,
For now.
Alcohol makes me feel like
My thoughts are not so
Cloudy.

Eros

I want to go on a
Living spree surrounded
By booze
And beautiful people.

Iota

Please
Let
Me
Go

Crescendo

I really want to have sex, I
Feel like it is something
That I need to do.
Hopefully it will be a good
Experience with a good
Person when the time is
Right.

Idiote

I have nothing to keep me around.
I am still here for the people
That love me,
I do not want them to think that
They could have saved
Me.

Eros

I want to go back to when
We both cared for each other
Before we called it dating
Back when it felt like
You could love me.

Iota

The only way I could
Get over you, is if
I chose to want to
Get over you.

Crescendo

I think smoking has
More health risks
Than
Drinking.

Idiote

I have lost everything,
Nothing is left for me,
I would like to die.

Eros

I am not who you fell for
I am not who you loved
I am not who you stopped loving
I am drained of all potential.

Iota

My thoughts are cloudy, I
Do not know what to do to
Get you back, I do not
Even know if I can want
You back.

Crescendo

I do not like that I was forced to
Quit drinking, for now, but
I am glad that I was
Made to feel that someone
Cares about me, is trying
To take care of me.

Idiote

I
Want
Alcohol
So bad.

Eros

Desperate
Dependent
Depressed
Not the type of D's people
Go out of their way to
Look for.

Iota

I do not even know where
I went wrong, so wrong
That I deserved hearing
You say that you stopped
Loving me.

Crescendo

I used to smoke because
It used to make me feel cool.
I do not like smoking, I do not
Like the smell or the taste.

Idiote

My prayers do not count,
I keep on talking to
God
But he wont talk back.

Eros

I hope that this is
Enough
To impress you
For now

Iota

Was I anything more
Than just a crush.

Crescendo

I like the distractions the
World has, your face
Was one hell of a distraction,
Such a heavenly sight.

Idiote

I tried to be good with God,
I couldn't help but be
Shit with myself.
I just want to be okay,
That is easier said than done.

Eros

People assume that I am not
Trying, that I do not try.
I believe that I deserve a
Trophy for the amount of
Effort I put into not dying
Everyday.

Iota

Do not
Speak
Do not
Listen

Crescendo

I talk too much about myself,
I should either be quiet more
Often and listen or I should
Ask them more questions about them-
selves.

Idiote

I am done
I want to die
There is nothing
here for me
Nothing I want
Nothing I need

Eros

I feel so lost right now,
I feel
Needy
And unwanted.

Iota

I do not know how to talk
To you without sounding
Pathetic
Desperate
Or stupid

Crescendo

I am
A
Psychopath,
You made me feel.

Idiote

I do not want to be killed
I want to kill myself
I want to deliver myself
To God.
I do not want anyone else
To take me there.
I want to take my life,
Away from everyone other than
Him,
God.

Eros

It crossed my mind that
You might have gone back to
Your ex, or you have someone
New, and I am still here
Writing about
You.

Iota

I know I am not pathetic,
Desperate, or stupid
But I can't help but
Feel that way.

Crescendo

I want my chest to feel
Something other than tired
And my heart to feel
Something other than
Weak.

Idiote

When I was lost, confused
And drunk you did not seem
To care, you did not seem
To be phased by what
I was going through

Eros

There are a lot of questions that
I wish to ask you, but I
Am afraid to know the
Answers.

Iota

I
Need
You
!

Crescendo

You could not save
Me from myself
And that is not
Your
Fault

Idiote

My heart hurts
I wish to feel something
Other than the constant
Pain
In my chest.

Eros

Iota

Drinking
Smoking
Girls
Boys.

I am sorry for being Crazy, I
Get really impulsive when I do
Not know what to do.

I hope that we will be able
To have an actual conversation
Real soon.

Crescendo

I am not a liar
Therefore
I do not
Lie

Idiote

Sometimes I feel that
I can die
And no one will care.
That feels nice.

Eros

I want to do what I want,
When I want and not
Feel like I have to share
What I am doing with
You.

Iota

No
More
Small talk

Crescendo

Do not talk
About
Yourself.

Idiote

I want to die
But I have not earned
That privilege yet.
Someday I will deserve
Death.

Eros

Writing about you coming
Back is hard because it is
Not a possibility that you
Are considering and I do
Not know if I would take
You back.

Iota

Go be yourself and
I wish that I can win
Your heart by being
Myself again.

Crescendo

I would love to feel pretty,
Attractive and wanted.
That might be the reason
I want to get fucked
So bad.

Idiote

Please make it
Stop
Please take away the
Pain.

Eros

You used to worry that
I would move on if things
End.
Look at you ending things
And moving on.

Iota

Someday my dreams will stop
Being dreams, they will
Either come true or I will
Forget.

Crescendo

There is a lot that you
Should know
But the time is not
Right.

Idiote

I wish that i wrote down
The sweet words I said to you,
I would have loved to see
Those words on paper.

Eros

Your tears are worth
Gold
Your smile is worth
The world.

Iota

When you hear me cry
Listen
When see a tear fall
Admire

Crescendo

I feel like I am losing my
Mind, it is getting harder to
Breath and my heart hurts.
I love you.

Idiote